陈东诗集

Collection of Chen Dong's Poems

汉英对照

Collection of Chen Dong's Poems
Chinese-English

陈 东 著
宋德利 译
Written by Chen Dong
Translated by Song Deli

易文出版社

陈东诗集

作者：陈　东
翻译：宋德利
插图：刘子楠　陈东
封面图案：陈滢卉
装帧设计：王昌华(Changhua Wang)

出版：易文出版社股份有限公司
www.iwingpress.com
admin@iwingpress.com
印刷：UADC Inc.
www.printandmat.com

版次：2016 年 8 月纽约第一版；2018 年 4 月第二次印刷
字数：20 千字
定价：$20.00
国际书号(ISBN)：978-1-940742-90-8

陈　东
Chen Dong

　　陈东（1936—），天津市人。天津市作家协会会员、天津作协文学院签约作家。曾出版诗集《湖边石子》和《凝神》。诗集《湖边石子》获天津市第十届文化杯"最佳诗集奖"。作品《廉价的糖果》被选入《2007年中国诗歌精选》；诗集《凝神》获天津市文化局举办的天津市第十九届"文化杯"全国鲁藜诗歌奖一等奖。

　　Chen Dong (1966—) was born in Tianjin. Member of Writers' Association of Tianjin. Published two collections of poems The pebbles by the lake and Attentiveness. Winner of "The best of poetry award" of The tenth cultural cup of Tianjin City. His Cheap candy was selected into A treasury of Chinese poetic gems of 2007. Winner of First Prize of National Lu Li Poetry Prize of the nineteenth Cultural cup of Tianjin.

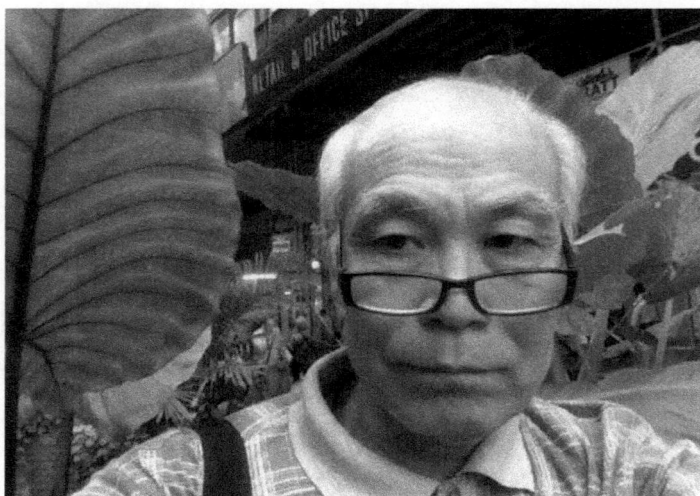

宋德利
Song Deli

宋德利（1944—），天津武清人。旅美双语翻译家。南开大学外文系毕业。南开大学、天津外院客座教授。曾任纽约美国中文电视编辑。翻译出版《聊斋志异》、《西游记》、《论语》、《道德情操论》等多种书籍。东西方艺术家协会翻译终身成就奖得主。

Song Deli (1944—) was born in Tianjin. Bilingual translator living in America. Graduated from the Foreign Language Department of Nankai University. Visiting professor of Nankai University and Tianjin Foreign Language College. Editor of Sino Vision in New York. Translated and published over 20 books including Strange Tales of a Lonely Studio, Journey to the West, The Analects of Confucius, The Theory of Moral Sentiments. Winner of Lifetime Achievement Award of Translation of the East-West Association of Artists.

目　录
Contents

序 言

个性诗人　灵性短诗
——谷 羽

　　诗人陈东，1966 年出生于天津市，多年从事诗歌创作。近年来出版了两部诗集《湖边石子》和《凝神》。现在，他从这两本诗集中精选出七十多首短诗，请资深翻译家宋德利先生译成英语，出版汉英对照的双语读本。这对于中外诗歌交流，是件很有意义的事情。

　　浏览陈东的诗集，会发现很多诗短小凝练，意象生动，富有灵性，耐人寻味。比如《湖边石子》，写得颇具个性：

　　　　　湖水蓝色
　　　　　天空蓝色
　　　　　湖边的石子坚韧
　　　　　几千年
　　　　　还不肯变成蓝色
　　　　　不知道石子
　　　　　怀着怎样的信念

　　湖是浩瀚的，天是辽阔的，湖畔石子渺小孤独，然而它坚韧而自信，不肯轻易改变自己的颜色，不随波逐流，彰显出独立不羁的人格与理念，这似乎是诗人的创作宣言。

　　又如《湖水》

　　　　　从湖水想到露珠
　　　　　从一只白鸟想到孤独

I

湖水能盛下多少露珠
就能盛下多少想你的苦

　　这是诗人在西藏工作期间，倾诉对妻子的思念。意
象清新，诗味隽永。诗人陈东耐得寂寞，亲近自然，常
常独自仰望山水，偶尔触发灵感，谱就诗篇，想象力丰
富而奇特，给他的诗增添了非凡的光亮和色彩。
　　同样抒发思念之情的《写信》，构思新颖别致：

我在火炉边给你写信
你收到后
要到暖和的屋子去读
因为我怕
你那地方太冷
降低了信的温度

　　写信人的心是热的，一般人都能想象得到，但"在
火炉边写信"，让书信也产生"温度"，则是独到的体
验，显示出诗人不懈的追求与创造性；而让收信人到"暖
和的屋子去读"，担心外面冷，"降低了信的温度"，
则在憨厚中透露出几分灵秀。
　　富有想象力的空灵之作似乎更多。请看《火车车
窗》：

火车车窗的灯光
在黑夜里滑过
像排列整齐的流星
不知道天上的流星里
是不是也坐着
疲惫的旅客

从夜晚火车车窗的灯光，联想到天上的流星也许不难，然而进一步把流星想象成列车，并且追问，那流星列车上是否也坐着"疲惫的旅客"，却是突发奇想的神来之笔。

《蝴蝶》只有短短的四行：

> 一把碎纸
> 高处撒下
> 你是唯一
> 往高处飞

诗中的意象"蝴蝶"，同样凸显出一种昂扬向上的精神。"蝴蝶"的翅膀承载着诗人的向往。这首诗的构思与《湖畔石子》有异曲同工之妙，立足于个性与环境的对比，从烘托与反差当中表现顽强的生命力。

诗人不仅拥有细致入微的观察力、想象力，他的嗅觉也异常敏锐，否则写不出《味道》这么细腻奇妙的作品：

> 风的味道来自浮萍
> 浮萍的味道来自河水
> 河水的味道来自游鱼
> 游鱼的味道来自腐泥
> 腐泥的味道来自岁月
> 岁月的味道呀
> 有些是眼泪的味道

七行诗"味道"出现了七次，但读者并不觉得重复累赘，"顶珠"手法的运用，形成行与行尾部与开头的连贯，增强了作品的节奏感与结构感。这样的诗洋溢着生活气息，又蕴涵哲理，让人百读不厌。

诗人并不局限于个人生活的小圈子，有时把目光投向社会，《玻璃》以含蓄的语言，表现人性的异化，角度新颖，思想颇有深度：

> 破碎以后
> 在围墙上
> 闪光
> 曾经那么害怕受伤
> 此刻
> 刀锋闪亮

曾经的脆弱者、受害者，竟然变成了防范者或权势者的帮凶，想想某些被贩卖的妇女，后来也成了人贩子，想想"为虎作伥"的成语，这首诗的确像围墙上的碎玻璃，令人望而生畏，心头震颤，不由得感到恐惧与寒冷。

陈东还有一首短诗《人与鸟》，耐人寻味：

> 人喜欢的鸟
> 关在笼子里
> 鸟喜欢的鸟
> 还在林子里

短诗的灵感，来自换位思考。善于从常见的生活现象中汲取诗意，言有尽，而意无穷，这样的诗歌，往往从物质层面上升到精神的空间，让人感悟，发人深思，因而具有更强的艺术感染力，自然也会更容易叩响读者的心扉。

诗歌，是用尽量少的语言，尽量小的篇幅，包容尽量多的内容，展现尽量深刻的意涵。陈东的诗是朝这样的方向努力，并且取得了可喜的成果。期待他不断进取，有更加精美深刻的佳作奉献给读者。

谷羽，1940 年出生，南开大学外国语学院教授，资深翻译家，天津市作家协会会员，俄罗斯圣彼得堡作家协会会员。主要译著有：《俄罗斯名诗 300 首》、《普希金爱情诗全编》、《普希金诗选》、《费特诗选》、《蒲宁诗选》、《茨维塔耶娃诗选》和三卷本的《茨维塔耶娃传记》。1999 年获俄罗斯联邦文化部颁发的普希金奖章。

Poet of character, short poem of spirituality
（preface）

Gu Yu

Poet Chen Dong was born in 1966. He has been engaged in poetry creation for many years. In recent years, he published two collections of poems Pebbles at the lakeside and Fixed attention.

Nowadays, he selected over seventy poems and invited senior translator Mr. Song Deli to translate them into English and formed a new bilingual collection named Collection of Chen Dong's Poems. It is an event of profound meanings for Sino-foreign poetry exchange.

If you skim through this collection of poems, you'll find many an excellent short poem. Refine and elegant with vivid images and spirit they afford for thought. I'd like to take Pebbles at the lakeside as an example of individuality:

Pebbles at the lakeside

The lake water is blue

The sky is blue

The pebbles at the lakeside are tough and tensile

For several thousand years

They've been reluctant to change the blue

No one knows

What sort of belief these pebble cherish

The lake is vast. The sky is spacious. The pebbles at the lakeside are tiny and lonely. Yet, they are firm, tenacious and self-confident. They refuse to change their color readily. They don't go with the stream. All these precisely display the human dignity and idea of independence and unruliness. It seems to be the creation declaration of the poet. Another instance is as follow:

The lake water

Think of dew drops from lake water

Think of loneliness from a white bird

Lake water can contain as many dew drops

As the bitterness I suffer when missing you

This is the story that the poet was pouring out of his missing to his wife when working in Tibet. The image is fresh and vivid; the lingering poetic charm is meaningful and thought-provoking. Poet Chen Dong is able to bear loneliness and close to nature. He often looks up at the mountains and down at the rivers. So long as his inspiration is occasionally ignited he would compose a poem. His imagination is rich and peculiar. This adds extraordinary light and colors to his poems.

One more example is Letter writing which also expresses the feelings of missing his wife. The design is novel and unique.

VI

Letter writing

I'm writing you a letter beside the stove
After getting it
Please read it in a warm room
Because I'm afraid of cold
Your place is cold, too
It may lower the temp of the letter

The heart of the letter writer is warm. This can be imagined nearly by every common people. But he wrote letters at the heatingstove and should let his letter generate temperature. This is really caused by his unique experience. This fully shows the unwavering pursuance and creation of the poet. He requested the receiver to "read it in a worm room". He worried it would be cold outside and "It may lower the temp of the letter". This shows that some intelligence and elegance were revealed from simplicity and honesty.

There seems to be more poems which are full of imagination and intangible spirit. Please read The Train window:

The Train window

The lamplight of the train
Slipped over in darkness
Just like the shooting stars in good order
Don't know among the shooting stars in the sky
If or not some tired passengers
Are also sitting in there

He associated the shooting stars in the sky from the lamplight coming out from the train window in the evening. This may not be very difficult. But he goes further to imagine that the shooting stars are the very train he took. And then he asked whether or not there were also some tired passengers sitting in the train of shooting stars. This is really a stroke of genius which comes from a sudden peculiar imagination.

Butterfly has only four short lines:

Butterfly

A handful of scraps of paper
Are scattered down from a high place
Yet you're the only one
To fly up

The image of the poem – butterfly also precisely displays a high spirit. The wings of the butterfly carry what the poet yarns for. Compared with The pebbles at lakeside, the conception of these two poems are different in approach but equally satisfactory in result. They are all established in the basis of comparison between personality and environment so as to express a dogged vitality from contrast and hongtuo, namely, add shading around an object to make it stand out.

The poet not only has an ability of meticulous observation and imagination but also enjoys an extremely sharp olfactory sensation. Or, he cannot write such an exquisite fantastic poet Taste.

Taste

The taste of wind comes from duckweeds
The taste of duckweeds comes from river water

VIII

The taste of river water comes from swimming fish

The taste of swimming fish comes from rotten mud

The taste of rotten mud comes from times

O, the taste of times

A part of it is to be the very taste of tears

The word of taste appears seven times in seven poetic lines. But readers do not feel reiteration and cumbersomeness at all. Why? The usage of thimble way created coherence, namely, the tail of the line before links the head of the line behind. This strengthened either the rhythm sensation or the composition sensation. The poems of this kind not only run over with vitality but also contain philosophy, and therefore, they can make readers feel that they are worth reading a hundred times indeed.

The poet never confines himself in a small circle of personal life. Sometimes, he casts his vision to the society. Glass expresses, with implicit language, the alienation of human nature. His point of view is novel and his thought is filled with profundity.

Glass

After being broken

On the bounding wall

You're sparking

You once madly feared being wounded

Yet at this moment

You're like a blade point glistening

Some people were once victims and vulnerable. But later they became defenders or even the accomplices of persons of power and influence. Let's think that some women were sold but later they should become human traders, too. Let's think the Chinese idiom -play the jackal to the tiger (help a villain do evil). What is said in this poem is really like the glass fragments on the bounding wall. When seeing them, people would get terrified and feel horrible and chilly with their hearts shuddered.

Chen Dong has another short poem Man and Bird, which affords for thought.

Man and Bird

The bird loved by man
Is closed in cage
But the bird loved by bird
Is still in forest.

The inspiration of this short poem comes from trans positional consideration. The poet is good at drawing poetic flavor, which can get the result of words being limited yet meanings being boundless. The poems of this sort usually enhance themselves to spiritual space from material level, and by way of this they can make people think deeply and enlightened. This, therefore, possesses stronger artistic infection. It, naturally, can more easily get resonance from readers.

Poetry uses as few words as possible, uses as short length as possible but contain as many contents as possible and displays as profound meanings as possible. Chen Dong's poetry is marching just toward this direction and he has already achieved delightful successes. We expect him to make progress constantly and have more exquisite poems to provide to the readers.

Note:

Gu Yu was born in 1940. A professor of the Foreign Language College of Nankai University. Senior translator. Member of Tianjin Writers Association. Member of Writers Association of St. Petersburg, Russia. His main translations: Three Hundred Russian Famous Poems, Complete Works of the Love Poetry of Pushkin (Пушкин), Collection of Poems of Pushkin, Collection of Poems of Feite (Фет), Collection of Poems of Bunin (Бунин), Collection of Poems of Tsvetaeva (Цветаева) and three book edition of Biography of Tsvetaeva. Winner of Pushkin Gold Award given by Ministry of Culture of Russian Federation in 1999.

好的风景

从外面看
半面墙都是窗户
屋里
一半都是床
连盖房子的砖都是半块半块的

在这样的家里
也可以看外面好的风景
可以看
圆的大的月亮

The good scenery

Look from outside,
Half wall is full of windows.
In the room,
Half is filled with beds.
Even bricks for house-building are half ones.

In this sort of families,
Good scenery outside can be watched.
The big round moon
Can be watched, too.

秋 夜

秋夜
很多蟋蟀叫
那就是蟋蟀在叫

只有一只蟋蟀叫
那是秋天在叫

Autumn night

Autumn night,
A lot of crickets are chirping.
They're crickets that are chirping.
Only one cricket is chirping.
It's autumn that is crying.

森林里

森林里
树是被安静抻长的
颜色是被安静加重的
傻傻地站在树下
每走一步
都会把整个森林的安静
搅动

In the forest

In the forest

Trees are quietly stretched longer

Colors are made darker peacefully

Silly standing under trees

Each step I take

Will have the tranquility of the whole forest

Stirred

秋天的风声

秋天的风声
遥远
远到了
在心的那一边

Wind sound in autumn

Wind sound in autumn
Is far
So far
In other side of heart

从平房搬到楼房

从平房搬到楼房
东西都搬走了
只剩下开满花坛的月季花
没法带走
它们开得正旺
就像我们在这里度过的时光

Move from bungalow to storied house

Move from bungalow to storied house
Everything was moved away
Only China roses left all over the flowerbed
No way to take them away
Cause they're fully booming
Like the time we spent here

踩着月光

踩着月光
如履薄冰
小心翼翼
怕被月光滑倒
踩着树的影子
不知道哪一根是树的尾巴
怕它突然一声惊叫

Tread on moonlight

Tread on moonlight
As if on thick ice
Carefully
Lest be slid down by moonlight
Tread on tree shadows
Not knowing which one is tree tail
Lest it should give a sudden scream

雪

白天的碎片
变成雪飘落下来
黑夜里
屋前屋后
落了一地的白天
有几片白天落在我的身上
好像可以弥补
白天里失去的遗憾

Snow

The fragments of day time

Have become snowflakes falling down

In the dark night

Before or behind the house

Day time fell on the ground all over

A few pieces of day time fell on my body

As if able to make up

The sorry lost in the day time

纳木错

车开到可以看见纳木错的山口
"看，纳木错"

"在哪儿？
没看见啊"

"仔细看
那不就是吗，
你顺着天空往下看……"

"哦，看到了
原来它和天空的蓝色融在一起
只有仔细分辨
才能把它从天空里分出来"

Namucuo

The car stopped at the mountain pass where Namucuo -
can be seen.
"Look, Namucuo."

"Where?
Can't see."

"Look carefully,
Isn't that there?
Look down from the sky ......"

"Oh, I see it
It's melted with the blue of the sky.
Only by carefully distinguishing
Can you separate it from the sky."

花　猫

很多年前
每天早晨学习
读书记笔记
花猫在窗外叫
打开窗户放它进来
它就趴在台灯下面
趴在我的一堆书上睡觉
有时我从它的身下拿一本书
它还不乐意地叫

后来它没有了
回想起来
那段时间我没有好好照顾它
有时还烦它
它丢了
心里一直难过
不知道该怎样做
才能安慰它
希望找到它的魂
听说它有九个魂
哪怕能找到其中一个
能好好安慰
好好爱它
也能减轻我心里的愧疚和遗憾

The spotted cat

Many years ago
I studied every morning
Read and took notes
The spotted cat cried outside the window
I opened the window and let it enter
It laid under the table lamp
And on a pile of my books sleeping
Sometimes I took a book from under its body
It cried unwillingly

It disappeared later on
Recalling
That period of time I took no good care of it
Sometime I once bothered it
It was lost
I've been sad in my heart
Not know what to do
To comfort it
Hope to find its soul
I was told it has nine souls
Even if able to find only one
Able to comfort it
And love it
Regret and sorry in my heart can be eased

空 白

冬天是空白的
春天
长出花花草草

心里是空白的
春天
什么也没有长出来

Blank

Winter blank
Spring
Grass and flowers came out

Blank in heart
Spring
Has not come out

牧

莒草横斜的土坡上
一件旧棉袄的背影
斜插一支放羊鞭
看不见那土坡下
有几只羊
我猜想
他放牧的是心灵

Herd

On the slope with reed crosswise
The back view of an old cotton padded jacket
Obliquely insert a sheepherding whip
Can't see below the earth slope
How much sheep
I guess
It's soul that he herds

秋

（一）
把一只透明的鸟
放飞在天空一样的心里

（二）
天空在每一个季节生长
秋天长到最高
连心里的天空
也留下了太多的空旷

Autumn

(I)
Let a transparent bird
Fly into the heart-like sky

(II)
The sky grows in every season
When autumn grows to its highest altitude
Even the inner sky
Leaves too much hollowness

夜 雨

打在窗二
挂钟声停了
打在瓦上
瓦深了
天黑了
没人看得清了
远处苇荡没有声
近处苇叶沙沙响
浇灌后的夜更静了
开始生长蛙声了

Night rain

Beat window
Wall clock stops
Beat tiles
Tiles become deeper
It's getting dark
No one can see clearly
Far reed marshes soundless
Near reed leaves are susurrating
After watering, night goes quieter
Croaking starts growing

味 道

风的味道来自浮萍
浮萍的味道来自河水
河水的味道来自游鱼
游鱼的味道来自腐泥
腐泥的味道来自岁月
岁月的味道呀
有些是眼泪的味道

Tastes

The tastes of wind come from duckweed
The tastes of duckweed come from river water
The tastes of river water come from swimming fish
The tastes of swimming fish come from rotten mud
The tastes of rotten mud come from time and tide
Oh, the tastes of time and tide
Some is the tastes of tears

乡村雨后

你聆听
雨后的夜晚
一镰旧月
裁开云朵的信封
把满窗的夜空
写上我的投寄
又胆怯地匆忙隐去了字形
不知你是否读懂
一只夜鸟
远远地从你窗前掠过
那是我
飞快地署名
那是一只归家的孤鸿
抖落几滴
冰凉的雨星

The courtry after rain

You listen
Night after rain
An old crescent
Opens the envelop of cloud
Write the night sky filling the window

Into what I mail
But cravenly and hurriedly hide the character patterns
Don't know whether you understand
A night bird
Distantly sweeps past before your window
That's my
Fast signature
That's a lonely swan goose returning home
Shakes off a few drops of
Ice-cold rain star

云 影

山坡上黑绿色的草
那是云的影子
掠过头顶
沿着原野上的晴朗
远行
一团白晰的云朵
影子才这样纯净
和我一起呼吸草原的气息
你远去就不能回来
那路过这里的早已不是你

Cloud shadows

The dark green grass on the hillside
Are cloud shadows
Skim over my head
Along the fairness on grassland
Fly for a long journey
Only a white cloud
Can have such a pure shadow
And take the breath of grassland together with me
Since you go far and then can't turn back
The one passing here hasn't been you any longer

距 离

从寂寞到不寂寞
从煎熬到静静地想你
是一段怎样的距离
像闪电与灯光的距离
闪电死得太快
灯光慢慢地消耗自己

从我到你
从心里想说的话到你的耳朵
是一段怎样的距离
像残雪与阳光的距离
雪不肯融化阳光又不愿离去

Distance

From loneliness to un-loneliness
From torment to quietly thinking of you
What sort of a distance is it?
Like the distance between lightning to lamp light
Lightning dies too quickly
Lamp light consumes itself slowly

From me to you
From my inner words to your ears
What sort of a distance is it?
Like the distance from un-melted snow to sunshine
Snow reluctantly melts sunshine and is unwilling to leave

简单的爱直到老年

窗上冻出的霜花
是美丽的少女

淌下平和的水滴
是她的老年

娴静的你
到了老年也一样的祥和吧

最幸福的是拥有老年时的平静
像最初一样的单纯

像淡淡的
捉摸不定的亲情

Simple love until getting old

The frostwork frozen on the window
Is a beautiful maid

Flow down mild water drops
They're her agedness

You're gentle and quiet
Can you still be so kind in old age?

The happiest thing is to enjoy calmness in old age
Like the early purity

Like the light
Unpredictable Kinship

蝉

天已经黑了
蝉还在叫
四野空寂

心里叫你的名字
像一只不知疲倦的蝉

Cicada

It was already dark
Cicadas are still chirping
The vast expanse of open ground is quiet and deserted

Call your name in my heart
Like an inexhaustible cicada

测量风

美人蕉花淡黄色的一团阳光
在靠墙的花圃中
树的影子投在墙上
作美人蕉花的背景
花轻轻晃动
背后的树影不动
风的大小
刚好在花和树影之间

Wind measurement

The light-yellow canna like a ball of sunshine

She's in the flower nursery leaning on the wall

Tree shows cast onto the wall

To be the background of the canna

Flower is lightly wagging

The tree shadows don't move

Powerful or weak

The wind strength is just between flower and tree shadow

写 信

我在火炉边给你写信
你收到后
要到暖和的屋子去读
因为我怕
你那地方太冷
降低了信的温度

Letter writing

I'm writing you a letter beside the stove
After getting it
Please read it in a warm room
Because I'm afraid of cold
Your place is cold, too
It may lower the temp of the letter

阳 光

阳光晒热了天葬台上的石头
鹰的目光冰冷依旧

Sunshine

Sunshine heated the stones on celestial burial platform
Eagles' eyes are still ice-cold

一大盆五颜六色的湿衣服

一大盆五颜六色的湿衣服
放在路边一个旧平房的门前
两个小女孩吃力地抬着一桶水过来
慢慢倒进大盆里
想起小时候常看着这样的情景
每天就生活在这样的氛围中
那时候心里特别安静

A big basin of colorful wet clothes

A big basin of colorful wet clothes
In front of the door of an old bungalow by the roadside
Two girls are laboriously carrying over a bucket of water
Then slowly poured into the big basin
Remember I often saw such scene when young
I lived in this sort of atmosphere every day
At that time I felt quite peaceful

一条小路

雅鲁藏布江对面有一条小路
那是骑马人的小路
是生长民歌的地方

柏油路跑了一天
江那面的小路还没有断

望一望对岸
就像从现在望一望古代

阳光到对岸就古老了
目光到对岸就年轻了
风到对岸就停了
时间到对岸就放慢了

吉普车到一座城市了
小路到大山深处了

A path

There's a path on the other side of the Yarlung Zangbo River
That's a path used by saddle-men
That's a place where folk songs grow

The asphalt road ran a day
The path on the other side of the rive hasn't been broken

Look at the other side
As if look at the ancient time from now

Sunshine will be age-old when it gets to the other side
Vision will be young when it gets to the other side
Wind will be stop when it gets to the other side
Time will be slow down when it gets to the other side

The jeep reached a city
The path reached the depth of the mountain

不想知道

地图上一个一个的圆点
一点一点击破
这个地球的神秘
所有童话般遥远的地方
都被安上了不合适的地名

当我沉浸在荒凉中
看见牧羊人的微笑
不想知道地名

当我像阳光一样
看着湖面上各种各样的水鸟
不想知道地名

当我在紧挨着天空的悬崖上
望着下面几座山峰的山顶
不想知道地名

当我面对你明朗的微笑
不想知道
你心里想什么

Don't want to know

The dots on the map
Beat the globe's mysteries broken
One by one
All the fairy-tale-like far places
Were given improper place name

When bathed in desolation
I saw the smile of the shepherd
I don't want to know the place name

When I, like sunshine, look at
Varied water birds on the surface of the lake
I don't want to know the place name

When, on the cliff near the sky, I
Look at the tops of the several peaks below
I don't want to know the place name

When facing your clear smile
I don't want to know
What you think of in your mind

在桦树林

到处是干净的枯树叶
一举一动都是悉簌的声音

别处的空气是飘来的
这里的空气是新长出来的

每一片薄薄的叶子
都有四季那么深

In the birch grove

There're clean withered tree leaves everywhere
Every movement of theirs is a scuttling and the rustling

The air of the other-places is to waft here
But the air here is to grow out

Every thin leave
Is deep as the four seasons

晨

月季花垂下枝头
不知是露水重了
花重了
还是香气重了

Morning

The Chinese rosedroops its branch
Do not know if the dew is heavy
Or the flower is heavy
Or the fragrance is heavy

玛旁雍错

不论怎样望
这里只有两种颜色
白色的雪
和蓝色的湖水

颜色锋利
天空都不敢向它靠近
地平线更躲得
看不见踪影

红色的月季花瓣上
是红色的极致
粉色的月季花瓣上
是粉色的极致
黄色的月季花瓣上
是黄色的极致
你是蓝色的极致
你是白色的极致

向你走近
站在湖边的白雪上
蓝色浸透了我
白色浸透了我
清纯的气息浸透了我
想起童年印象最深的一次感激
也不如此时对你的感激

Mapangyongcuo

No matter how to look
Here're only two colors
The white snow
And the blue lake water

The colors are so sharp
That even the sky dare not go close to them
And the horizon line hid itself
Nowhere in sight

On the petals of red Chinese roses
Lies the red extremity
On the petals of pink Chinese roses
Lies the pink extremity
On the petals of yellow Chinese roses
Lies the yellow extremity
You're the blue extremity
You're the white extremity

Walk close to you
Stand on the white snow at the lake side
Blue color soaked me
White color soaked me
Pure smell soaked me
Remember that the most impressive thank in childhood
Is no better than the present thank to you

蟋 蟀

蟋蟀拨打着电话
不停地拨
耐心地等

不知道号码前
是哪个区号

那个区号
代表了怎样一片痴情的土地

Cricket

The cricket is dialing the phone
Dials it on and on
And wait patiently
Without knowing before the number
Is which area code

That area code
Represent what sort of a love-struck land

逆光的影子

大雨后的黄昏
越野车溅起积水
背着孩子的母亲停下来
紧靠路边望着飞快的车轮和身边的积水

身后是饱满的小河和湿重的青稞
车子慢慢经过她的身边
才急着远去
逆光的影子掩进黄昏

Backlighting shadow

At dusk after a heavy rain

The off-road vehicle is splashing the ponding

The mother with a kid on her back stopped

Close to roadside looking at the rapid car wheels and
the ponding beside her

Behind her are the plump little river and wet heavy
highland barley

The vehicle slowly goes by her side

And then rapidly runs away

The backlighting shadow enters the dusk

扳道工

黑色的寒冷
总是带着呼号的声音
冷得发出两道幽幽的光
伸向天边的远处
你喷薄的热气
生成另一个不再寒冷的道岔
你手上的温热
连接着远方的一座春城

The switchman

The black cold

Always bears the calling sound

So cold that it se-ds out two lines of faint light

Stretching to the ⁻ar end of the sky

Your boundless hot gas

Produced anothe⁻ turnout not cold any longer

The tepidity in your hands

Is linked with a far spring city

黑 暗

我爱你的黑暗
你的不可及的深远
黑暗多么光滑，多么温暖
你是我深爱又不能接近的人
你是在远处微笑又转身离去的人
你让我感到亲切却又被一道线隔开
一道可近可远又紧紧贴着我的黑暗

Darkness

I love your darkness

Your "found and lasting" can't be reached

How smooth, how warm the darkness is

You're the person I deeply love but can't be close to

You're the person smiling far off and then turning-back -
and leaving

You make me feel cordial but to be separated by a line

A line of darkness near or far but close to me

廉价的糖果

喜欢去小时候常去的光线黯淡的旧商店买东西
一进店门
就闻到一种小时候印象很深的味道
说不清是糖果的
调料的
还是制作粗糙的糕点的味道
黑乎乎的旧木柜台
盛糖果的圆玻璃瓶子
小时候仰望的瓶子里的好看的糖果
现在低头俯视着
这些简易制作包装的廉价的糖果
里面的甜从没有廉价过
生活中的甜
我还像小时候一样仰望

Cheap candy

Love to go shopping in the dark old store where I often -
went in childhood
After entering the door
I smelt out a flavor giving me deep impression when young
Can't tell whether t's the flavor of the candy
Or of the spices
Or of the smell of the coarsely made cakes
The black old wooden desk

The round glass bottles to contain the candy
The good-looking candy in the bottles which I often looked -
up at when young
Is lowering its head and looking over
These cheap candies with simply made and packed
But the inner sweetness has never been cheap
The sweetness in life
I look up at it still like how I did in my childhood

狼的嚎叫

像一块飞到天上的布
把星星擦得更亮了
在群星的逆光里
远山的剪影分出了几层
层叠中的几点烛光
像遗落的几颗星星
我不再赶路
路走不完
牛粪炉熄了
两床旧被
挨着我的一面热了
也暖不过外面的冷
窗外没有了过车的声音
前面没有了住处
今夜
我住在没有灯的土屋里
成了高原的一部分
一个人
却是最不孤单的时候
从没有过的平静
从没有过的满足
从没有过的与自然亲近的荣耀
今夜
黑暗离我最近
仿佛是逼着我
变成一颗发光的寒星

Howl of wolf

It's like a cloth flying into the sky
And wiped the stars brighter
In the backlighting of the stars
Distant mountain outline were separated into several layers
Among the layers a few points of candle light
Are like a few stars left over there
I no longer hurry on with my journey
The road is too long to finish
The cow dung stove was put out
Two old quilts
Becomes warm in the side against me
But it cannot withstand the cold outside
There's no sound of passing vehicles
Nowhere to live in front
Tonight
I live in the earth house without lamp
And thus became a part of the plateau
One person only
But it's not the most lonely moment
It's the calmness I've never enjoyed
It's the satisfaction I've never had
It's the glory I've never had which is natural, near and dear
Tonight
Darkness is near me the most
As if it forces me
To turn into a shining cold star

逛早市

遍地的商品
连阳光一起卖给你

遍地的鲜花
连春风一起卖给你

今天好心情最廉价
今天微笑最便宜

Stroll in early market

Goods are all over the ground
Sell them to you together with sunshine

Flowers are all over the ground
Sell them to you together with spring wind

Today's good mood is cheapest
Today's smile is at the lowest price

以 为

以为树叶落了
可以看见蝉
以为河水流干
可以看见鱼
以为时间久了
可以忘记

| think

| thought the leaves had fallen
So | could see cicadas
| thought the river water drained off
So | can see fish
| thought it took a long time
So | could forget

窗 外

雨声比钟表声响得急
与我争夺时间
旧木窗已破损
还少了一块玻璃
宿舍里的时间
都是寂寞的时间
全都给你了
尽管拿云
心里的时间
那些幸福时间
不会给你

Outside the window

Rain sound is more rapid than that of clock
Fight with me to seize time
The old wooden window has been broken
A piece of glass has disappeared
The time in dorm
Is all the lonely time
All has been given to you
You just take it away
The time in heart
That happy time
Cannot be given to you

窗台上

土坯屋
旧木窗
大大的窗台
晾晒着
孩子用泥巴做的小人
这些小人的成长
就是慢慢地
恢复它
黄土的颜色

On window sill

House made of sun-dried mud brick
Old wooden window
Very big window sill
To dry
The little persons made of mud by kids
The growth of these small persons
Is to recover the color
Of yellow soil
Slowly

闪 亮

趴在草地上
借着阳光
侧脸看一片草丛
鲜嫩闪亮的是虫草
花蝴蝶落在一地的枯树叶上
闪亮的是它彩色的翅膀
这些小小的安静的亮光
像茫茫人海中
一个含蓄腼腆的微笑
都是每天流失的
无数个不经意的
瞬间

Glisten

Lie on the grassland
With help of sunshine
Turn face aside and look at grass-cluster
What is glistening s worm grass
Colorful butterflies fell on the withered leaves all over
the ground
The colorful wings are glistening
The qu et light

Is like a coy smile
In the vast sea of people
It's uncountable moment which lapses every day
It's a causal
Moment

稻子熟了

一片片渐渐变黄的稻田
稻穗饱满
麻雀在上面飞飞停停
在没有稻子的地方
麻雀们飞得又快又远
嗖嗖地总在赶时间
在稻田里，它们的时间一下子富有了
也不去别的什么地方
飞得慢，飞几下就停下来
好像身子重得飞不动了似的
鸽子、喜鹊，大大小小的鸟
在稻田周围，在田埂上
在挺拔的稻子的边上
都来和稻穗说话
稻株从一开始就生出根须
株旁边不断地生出小枝来
现在成熟饱满，长出薄如蝉翼的稻芒
它从没想过扑闪稻芒让自己飞起来
就这样默默地献出自己
冬天，稻田里只剩下短短的稻茬
再没有鸟来和它说话
黄昏的时候，村子里升起炊烟
空气里弥漫着燃烧稻草的香味
又干又硬的稻茬向着天空微笑
好像看见
儿女们都来看它

Rice is ripe

Pieces of paddy fields going yellow gradually
Ears of rice are plump
Sparrows fly above, stop-and-go
In places without rice
They fly rapidly and far
Whooshing to catch time
In the padded fields, they've plenty of time
So they won't go other places
Very slow, fly a few moments and stop
As if their bodies are too heavy to fly
Pigeons, magpies, varied birds, big or small
Around the padded fields, on ridges
Beside the tall and straight rice
All come to have talks with rice ears
Rice stems started to grow root hair from the very beginning
Small branches growing out beside stems
They've plump and ripe, growing out awns thin as cicada wing
The small branches have never thought to press awns and fly up
They're quietly dedicating themselves
In winter, only stubbles are left in the padded fields
No birds come to talk with them anymore
At dusk, cooking smoke is rising above the village
The sweet smell of burning rice straw spread in the air
The dry and hard stubbles are smiling to the sky
As if saw
Their sons and daughters come to see them

雨 后

雨后
山、森林，崎岖的山路都是湿的
松树还在滴水
汽车在泥路上颠簸
星星在夜空中跳舞
四周都是湿的
只有目的地是干的
目的地在远处
连整个季节的目的地
也在远处
从天空蔓延到四周的星星
明明没有淋到雨
竟然也是这样水灵灵的
我站在黑暗的孤岛上
四周是星星的大海

After rain

After rain
Mountains, forests, rugged mountain road are wet
Pines trees have water dripping down
Car jolts on the muddy road
Stars dance in the night sky

Surrounding is wet
Only destination is dry
Destination is far away
Even the destination of this season
Is far away, too
From the sky to the surrounding stars
They're precisely not drenched by rain
But they should be so fresh
I'm standing on the dark lonely islet
The surrounding is the sea of stars

沾满了泥的鞋子

下完雨
从果园回来
鞋子上沾满了泥
在墙角放了两天
泥成了白色
鞋已经干了，只是
对果园的印象
还是湿的

Shoes fully stained with mud

After rain
I come back from the orchard
My shoes are full stained with mud
They are put in the wall corner for two day
Mud became white
Shoes are already dry, only
My impression to the orchard
Is still wet

山的暗影

山的暗影
在星星与灯光之间
星星和灯光都在密集地凑热闹
都在引以自豪地闪亮
只有山影黑沉沉地
好像比星星还远

The mountain shadow

The mountain shadow
Is between stars and lamp light,
Stars and lamp light are joining in the fun, thick and fast
They're glistening proudly
Only mountain shadow is pitch-dark
It seems further than stars

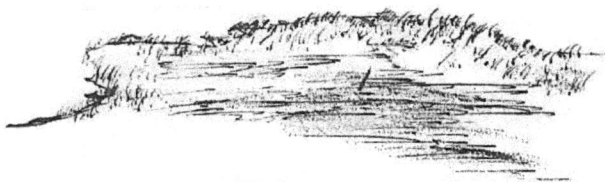

门前的桃花

门前的桃花
照亮了院墙和铁门
它是从开满野桃花的山谷里来的
那里白天自由灿烂
晚上也会冷和孤单

这家院子里住着一个太阳一样的人
野桃花想白天和夜里都能和他靠近
野桃花用每一朵桃花大声地喊他
他却关着门
不说一句温暖的话

Peach blossoms in front of the door

The peach blossoms in front of the door
They lightened the courtyard wall and the iron door
Coming from the valley filled with wild peach blossoms
The day there is free and brilliant
But at night it can be cold and lonely, too

A sun-like man lives in the yard of this family
The wild peach blossoms want to go close to him day and night
The wild peach blossoms want to call him loudly with every flower
But he keeps the door closed
Without saying even a single warm word

剥 豆

夜雨过后
天打开了
像剥开豆荚
里面
结满了星星

Stripping beans

After the night rain
The sky is opened
Like to strip off the pods
Inside
It fully set stars

海没有了

海没有了
这么大的海，
这么深厚的感情
说没有就没有了，
曾经蓝色的大海，
曾经以为你永远都在，
曾经那么亲，在一起，
说说笑笑的大海，
没有了。
真希望，
失去的人，失去的感情，
像涨潮一样地
回来。

The sea vanished

The sea vanished.
So big a sea,
So deep feelings,
They vanished suddenly.
Here was once a blue sea,
Once thought you would be here forever.
Once so close, being together,

The talking and laughing sea,
Vanished.
I really wish
The people vanished and the feelings lost
Would come back
Like flood tide

成功在于勇实。闻名的

获得全世界的不朽

秘密

——巴尔扎克

花的善良

所有的人都反对我
所有的人都讨厌我
院子里的花
并没有背过脸去

The kindness of blossom

All people oppose me
All people are sick of me
The blossoms in the courtyard
Didn't turn away

美发厅

在街边的美发厅里理发
闭着眼睛
听到了门外的雨声
有人开门
湿的气息已经进来了
带着清新的香气
拖着长长的身子
在屋里转悠
谁来为她美发
梳理湿润的风

Hair salon

I had haircut in the hair salon by the street
With my eyes closed
I heard the rain sound outside the door
Someone opened the door
Wet air already came in
With fresh fragrance
Pulling long body
Sauntering in the room
Who will give her hair-dress
And comb the wet wind

我的诗在为我流泪

我没有眼泪从不流泪
可我的诗好像饱含着泪水
隐隐约约地在远处
在没有人看到的地方
在安静的时候
我的诗泪水喷涌

眼泪像有雨的云彩
在理解我的人心上飘
一场暴雨
说下就下

My poems shed tears for me

I've no tears and never shed tears
But my poems seem to be filled with tear
Faintly in a distant place
In a place which cannot be seen by anyone
When being quiet
Tears gush out from my poems

Tears seem to be cloud with rain
Drifting over the heart of anyone can well understand me
A storm
Comes at anytime

小学校

走进教室
抚摸发黑的坑洼不平的墙皮
抚摸刻画得乱七八糟的桌椅
我走近你
却不能走近岁月

Primary school

Walk into the classroom
Stroke the hollow dark wall surface
Stroke desks and chairs carved rough-and-tumble
I walked close to you
But I cannot walk close to time and tide

牧羊女

峡谷里流不完的雪水
冰凉
不能化成暖流
就像思念
无法温暖

越来越远的目光
是
一生的收藏
心里装得下一座雪山
雪山跟着我走
心里装不下你
在土屋前
不跟我走

The shepherdess

The endless snow water in the valley
Is ice-cold
It cannot be turned into warm current
Like missing
Which cannot be warm

The further and further vision
Is
The collection of one's life
Mind can contain a snow mountain
The snow mountain follows me
Mind cannot contain you
In front of the earth house
It doesn't follow me

心越来越坚硬

心
越来越坚硬

童年时的心
本来有一块
特别温柔的部分
被带走了

不论过多久
这块本来是我的
温柔的心
都被带着
带到远处
带到看不到我的地方

Heart is harder and harder

Heart
Harder and harde-

My heart in childhood
Originally had a part
Especially mild
But taken away

陈东诗集

No matter how much time passed
This mild heart
Belonging to me
Was taken
Far away
To a place where I can't see it

小院安静

不知道有多少虫子木匠
在默默地锯树
时常有木屑和虫子的壳
从树上落下来
掺杂着阳光的碎末
落了一地
木屑和虫壳可以扫起来
阳光的碎末却总也扫不干净
把扫起来的木屑和虫壳收在一起
打成纸浆
做成纸
在上面写的诗
一定会带着小院儿的静
虫子的叫声
和阳光的温暖

The little yard is quiet

Not know how many worm carpenters
Are quietly sawing trees
Bits of wood and worm shells
Often fell down from the trees
Mingled with the detritus of sunshine

Falling all over the ground
Bits of wood and worm shells can be swept up
But detritus of sunshine cannot be fully swept
Collect the bits of wood and worm shells swept up
And turned them into paper pulp
And paper
Write poems on it
It must bear the quietness of the little yard
And the cry of insects
As well as the warmth of sunshine

从冰上看水的花纹

从冰上看水的花纹
坚硬的冰里面
水的花纹柔软舒展
它们是凝固着的
春水的模样

从雨后水面上的浮萍
看流水的线条
越靠河岸
芦苇和杂草越茂密
浮萍和它们连在一起
下过雨的河面上
浮萍画出天然的图案
显示出河水流出夏天的痕迹

从拥挤的地铁里
看一张一张平静的脸
从人们的脸上
看大家的心里
都有一片开阔的藏北草原

Look at the water ripples from on the ice

From on the ice to look at water ripples
Under the hard ice surface
The water ripples soft and freely stretching
They're the solidified
Appearance of spring water

From the duckweeds on the water surface after rain
I saw the lines of flowing water
The closer they're to the river bank
The denser reeds and weeds are
Duck weeds are linked with them
On the river surface after rain
Duck weeds drew out natural designs
Showing the summer traces flowing from the river water

From the crowded subways
One can see every calm face
From people's faces
One can see that in people's hearts
There exists a vast grassland in North Tibet

城市里

城市里
一只飞动的麻雀
把墙垛子的一段干树枝
踩了下来
清脆地落在水泥地砖上
路过的老人
把那段干树枝
捡起来
放在树下有泥土的方框里
人和麻雀合作
让落叶归根
让干树枝回到自己的家

In the city

In the city
A flying sparrow
Treaded down a section of dry tree twig
From the wall pier
Onto the cement floor tile with a slight crackling sound
An old passersby
Picked up
That section of dry tree twig

And put it into the square frame with mud under the tree
Thru cooperation between human and sparrow
Fallen leaves returned to the roots
Dry tree twig returned to the tree

女儿第一次喊爸爸

女儿第一次喊爸爸
美妙的音乐
直达内心
好像本来就是我内心深处的东西
却在外面漂泊
现在刚刚回来
回到我心里的家
爸——爸——
短短的声音像爆竹的短短的引信
点燃的一瞬间
心里的快乐
嘭然炸响
幸福在内心的天空里
纷纷扬扬

Daughter calls papa the first time

My daughter called me papa the first time
Beautiful music
Directly reaches my inner heart
As if anything originally existing in the depth of my heart
But drifting outside
Now it's just come back
And returned in the home in my heart

Pa-pa
The short sound is like the short fuse of fireworks
In the flash to lighten it
My inner pleasure
Blasted loudly
Happiness are drifting profusely and disorderly
In the inner heart of the sky

人喜欢的鸟

人喜欢的鸟
关在笼子里
鸟喜欢的鸟
还在林子里

The bird loved by Human

The bird loved by human
Is in the cage
The bird loved by birds
Is in the forest

重

花坠弯了花枝
花重了
露水重了
还是香气重了

Heaviness

Flowers bended the sprays
The flowers became heavy
The dews became heavy
Or the fragrance became heavy

鸟 窝

冬天
树枝上的鸟窝
和树枝一样暗灰色
春天
树枝绿了
树枝上开出了梨花桃花
鸟窝还是暗灰色
不能变绿也不能开花
任凭周围变化
它保持淡定安静
保持内心的温暖

Bird nest

In winter
The bird nest on the tree branch
Is dark grey like the branches
In spring
The tree branches became green
Pear and peach flowers are in bloom on branches
But the bird nest is still dark grey
Unable to turn green and have flowers in bloom
No matter what may in the surroundings
It still keeps quietness
And the inner warmth

远处的灯

天渐渐黑了下来
远处的灯亮了
小小的一点点光亮
竟然敢和黑暗抗衡
想想自己
可有这样的勇气

The lamp far away

It's getting dark

The far light is on

The little dots of light

Should dare to contend against darkness

Think of myself

If I have this sort of courage

雪山蘸来天上的蓝色

雪山蘸来天上的蓝色
蓝色随着融化的雪水
沿着一条条小溪
流到湖水里
所以湖水的蓝这么轻
好像随时可以被风吹散

The snow mountain lets the blue in the sky come by dipping

The snow mountain lets the blue in the sky come by dipping it

Together with the melted snow water

The blue flows along the small brooks

Into the lake water

So the blue of the lake water is so light

As if it may be blown away at anytime

几张交通宣传画片

小时候的一天
外面下着雪
天特别的冷
我在潮湿的平房的小屋里
妈妈在做饭
家就这样一间小屋
小屋的一大半是一张床
我就在大床上呆着
时不时地望望窗外
玻璃上结着水汽
屋里的热气连窗子都模糊了
这样寂寞无聊的时候
父亲从外边回来
一身的雪花水汽
给我一叠画片
是宣传交通安全的画片
上面的人物都那么漂亮好看
交警，推自行车，穿着厚厚的一家人，雪天
这些画片让我浮想联翩
想象着马路上的样子
画里面的亲情让我热爱
这是我在百无聊赖中最好的读物
在家里的大床上读着这些画片
心里真是幸福

A few pictures of traffic publicity

One day in my childhood
It was snowing outside
It was particularly cold
I was in the small room of our wet bungalow
My mother was cooking
There was only such a small room in our family
The better part of the small room was occupied by a bed
I was sitting on the big bed
Looking out of the window every now and then
The moisture was frozen on the glass
The hot-gas in the room made the window dim and vague
In this lonely and boring moment
My father came back from outside
Wrapped in snow flakes and water vapor
He gave me a stack of pictures
About traffic safety publicities
The figures in them were very beautiful
Traffic police, bikes, the people of a family wearing thick -
clothes, snowy day
These pictures made me fall into a reverie
Imaging the appearance of the roads
I loved the family affection in the pictures
They were my best reading matters when I was overcome with boredom
Reading these pictures on the big bed at home
Was really my inner happiness

灰色的树

冬天的树变成了灰色
春天变成了绿色
不知道它的绿色藏在什么地方
砍树的人，剖开树，没有看到绿色
木匠一层一层地刨开
刨出一卷一卷的刨花
也没有找到绿色
或许树们自己也不知道
绿色的源头在哪儿
只是替老天爷把绿色呈现出来
一棵普通的树
也肩负着老天爷赋予的
神圣的使命

The grey trees

The trees in winter turned into grey
Spring has become green
Not knowing where the green hid itself
The tree-chopping man, cast the trees away, without seeing
the green color
The carpenter is planning layer by layer
And planed out wood shavings one reel after another

But he found no green color at all
Or maybe even the trees themselves don't know
Where the source of green color exists
They only show the green color for Heavens
An ordinary tree
Also shoulders the holy mission
Given by Heavens

草原上的风

草原上的风
在最低的地方生活
贴着地
贴着草
贴着牛粪
它没有形状
它的味道就反映了它的出身
也反映了它想飞上天的心
阳光因为它柔软
牛毛细雨因为它涌起波浪

外人只看到他的自由
只有牧羊人
知道它潮湿的心

在草原上露餐
望着远方
吃着凉饼子
天上下起牛毛细雨
它来到身边
我一下子就感觉到了
它是多么地孤独

The wind on the grassland

The wind on the grassland
Lives in the lowest place
Closely near the ground
Near the grass
Near the cow dung
It's shapeless
Its smell reflects its origin
And reflects its will of flying into the sky
Sunshine became soft because of it
The fine drizzling rain is up-rushing waves because of it, too.

The outsider saw his freedom
Only shepherds
Know its wet heart

Eating on the grassland
Looking at the distant place
Eating cold pancake
It was drizzling
It came to my side
I suddenly felt
How lonely it was

飞 鸟

飞鸟
在天空中孕育
出生
又在天空中
消失

它在空中飞的时候
天空
曾经是多么地高兴啊

The flying bird

The flying bird
Was bred and
Born in the sky
And vanished
In the sky, too

When flying in the sky
It
Was once very happy

相 约

冬天一来
河水就结冰
它们早就约好了

冬天越过三个季节
从远方赶来

表面上寒冷
可它的心里
是多么幸福啊

An appointment

When winter came
The river water was frozen into ice
They already had ar appointment

Winter came after crossing three seasons
From a distant place

Cold on surface
But in heart
It was so happy

拉萨郊外的树林

拉萨郊外
有一片树林
树林边有一条河
水平静地流着
一片叶子落到静静的水面上
又有一片叶子落下来
一切都是慢动作
这里的时间与世界无关
过得慢
慢得和小时候放学后等爸妈回家一样慢
慢得让人打哆嗦
慢得骨头发麻
慢得阳光都要变馊了
不知从哪儿来的几个钓鱼人
不发出一点声音
因为这里水太浅
一丝响动都会把鱼吓跑

The forest in the suburb of Lhasa

In the suburb of Lhasa
There's forest
And a river by the forest

The water is quietly flowing

A leave fell onto the quiet water surface

Another leave fell down

All actions were very slow

The time here has nothing to do with the world

The time goes slowly

Slow as I was waiting for my parents back home after school in
my childhood

So slow that people shivered

So slow that my bones were numb

So slow that sunshine turned sour

Several fishermen, no one knows where they came from

They don't send out any sound at all

Because the water here is shallow

Even a little bit of sound can frighten fish away

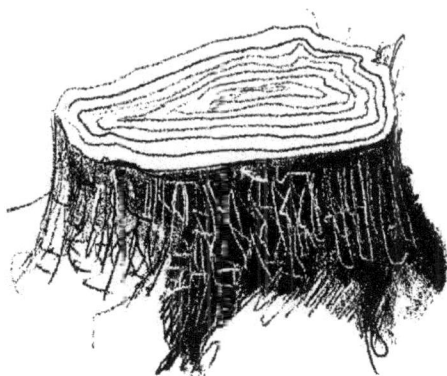

夏 天

(一)

啄木鸟把树抻长
蝉把夏天的每一秒抻长

(二)

圆叶的草在风中晃动
时时晾出背面的白色

(三)

雪山
在天空中裸泳

(四)

孩子站在向日葵下
抬头看见了它垂下的脸

(五)

农家小院的门灯很别致
灯卧进墙里

(六)

隔着厚厚的墙
也能闻见农家的气息

(七)

等着摊煎饼果子的时候
才注意看煎饼摊后面的那棵树

Summer

(I)

Woodpecker stretched the trees
Cicada stretched every minute of summer

(II)

The grass with round leaves is waggling in the wind
And shows the white on the rear side

(III)

The snowy mountains
Takes a naked bath in the sky

(IV)

Standing under the sunflower
The kid raised his head and saw its lopping face

(V)

The door lamp in the small Peasant Household is unique
The lamp lies in the walls

(VI)

Separated by the thick walls
The breath of farmers could be heard of

(VII)

When waiting to buy Chinese hamburger
I attentively looked at that tree behind the Chinese -
hamburger stand

关于月亮的三首小诗

（一）

上班不久的惠美
不顾转天要上班
和朋友们在沙漠上点篝火
唱歌，跳舞，喝大酒
月亮也很开心
大家都亡的时候
月亮也很孤独

（二）

扫一扫月亮
添加为好友
怕人笑话的傻话
可以发给它
虽然它从来没有回复
但是抬起头
就可以望一望它

（三）

彩色的焰火们飞上天
月亮只有白色
月亮黯然失色
焰火们哈哈笑着

月亮冷冷地
白了它们一眼

Three short poems about the moon

(Ⅰ)

Starting work not long ago,
Regardless he'll go on duty next day,
Hui Yong and his friends lit a bonfire on the desert
And sang, danced, drinking wine madly
The moon was also very delighted
When everyone was busy
The moon was also lonely

(Ⅱ)

Sweeping the moon
Add it as a good friend
The folly which he was afraid people would laugh at
Can be sent to it
Although it's not replied yet
But so long as raising head
You can look at it

（Ⅲ）

Colorful fireworks flew to the sky
The moon only has the white color
The moon was overshadowed
Fireworks laughed
The moon indifferently
Took a glance at them

窗下看书

窗下看书
书和笔记本由暗变亮
再由亮变暗
窗外的天空
云彩过去
书和笔记本就亮了
云彩来
又暗了下来
小时候在窗下写作业就是这样
重复到今天
太阳和云彩一样
照在书和笔记本上的光一样
通过眼睛
连到心里的暖意一样
只是
窗子不一样
面容不一样
房子不一样
小时候从变亮的书和作业本上
想到的是
田野上的阳光
现在
想到的
是田野的空旷和安详

Read books at the window

Read books at the window
Books and notebooks became bright from dark
But from bright to dark again
In the sky outside the window
Clouds passed
Books and notebooks were bright
Clouds came
And got dark
It was just like this when I did my homework at the window in my -
childhood
Repeated it till today
The sun was like the cloud
The light they were shining on books and that on notebooks
was the same
They were the same when passing thru the eyes
And then linking itself to the inner warmth
Only windows
Were different
Faces different
Houses different
What I thought when young from books and notebook
gradually getting light
Was the sunshine in the fields
But now
What I think about
Is the hollowness and sereneness in the fields

雪天的路

冬天
小饭店
桌上的火锅沸着水汽
白雾弥漫到了屋顶
窗外下着大雪
银白的路面和过往的骑车人
一位妇女推着自行车
后面坐着孩子
艰难地从窗前走过
仔细看
只是自行车艰难
孩子自然一脸舒服的样子
母亲是热汗蒸腾精神百倍的神情
这一带没有暖气
也许孩子的父亲还没有回来
也许她们回到的家现在还是干冷的
可是我忽然觉得
湿暖的小饭店
无论如何也暖不过
她们暂时干冷的家

The road in a snowy day

In winter
A slap-bang shop
The water is boiling in the chafing dish on the table
The rime fog pervading to the roof
A heavy snow is falling outside the window
Among the passing bike-riders on the silver-white road
A woman is pushing her bike
With two kids sitting behind her
She's walking difficultly in front of the window
Looking at her carefully
I found only bike being difficult
But the kids are very happy
The mother is in high spirit, though wet with sweat
There's no heating in this area
Maybe the father of the kids hasn't come back
Maybe it's very dry and cold when they're back at home
But I suddenly felt
The wet and warm slap-bang shop
Is by no means warmer than
Their temporarily dry and cold home

想　象

去阿里的路上
傍晚在小饭店吃饭
进来一个衣衫破旧的藏族孩子
怀里抱着一根木棍
当作琴
一只手拨动看不见的琴弦
微笑着
为我们唱歌
唱的歌词听不懂
问身边的藏族朋友
他唱的是不是自己悲伤的经历
朋友笑着说才不会呢
他唱的全是快乐的事
是他想象的
孩子抱着的木棍儿
是他想象中的琴
孩子的唱词
是他想象中的幸福
他圆圆的脸上
冒着火一样的红光
在这个漆黑的夜晚
屋外是满街的冷风
旁边是成片的雪山
所有这些寒冷
也没法扑灭
他想象中的温暖

Imagine

On the way to Ali
I had dinner in a slap-bang shop at dusk
There came in a Tibetan kid wearing shabby clothes
With a wooden stick in his arms
As a *qin*
A hand is playing the invisible string
Smiling
He's singing for us
The words of the song isn't understandable
Asking my Tibetan friends around
Whether he's singing about his own sorrowful experience
Friends smiled and said that was impossible
What he's singing about are all happy things
They're his imagination
The wooden stick in his arms
Is only the *qin* in his imagination
The song words of the kids
Are the happiness in his imagination
His round face
Is giving a fire-like red light
In this pitch-dark night
Cold wind is blowing the whole road outside the house
Beside the house there are boundless snowy mountains
These cold things cannot
Put out
The warmth in his imagination

清冷的目光

清冷的目光
滴在炽热的心上
吱吱沸响
整个世界
化成了一缕白烟

The light from cold eyes

The light from cold eyes
Dropped in the fiery heart
Boiling and squeaking
The whole world
Turned into a wisp of white smoke

白天是白色的时间

白天是白色的时间
夜里是黑色的时间
黄昏时的草茉莉花
是彩色的时间
白色的日子
黑色的日子
和你在一起
是彩色的日子

The day is the white time

The day is the white time
The night is the dark time
The jasmine flower at dusk
Is the colorful time
The white days
The dark days
Are together with you
Are colorful days